A Second Helping of PETER HARVEY'S SHEFFIELD

791 EVENING SHEFFIELD.

Most important of all, perhaps, it is the Sheffield of which many people have vivid memories, and in which younger people without their own memories, are deeply interested.

Without getting philosophical about it, I can't agree with people who say you should never look back, only forward. Certainly, no-one should spend most of his or her time looking back, but I have an abiding interest in Sheffield, and that includes how it looks today, how it will look in the future, and how it looked in the past, and it seems to me that all three periods are inextricably linked. It is only possible to judge properly if a street or an area has been improved by change if you are aware of how it used to be.

Besides, people are always interesting, in the way they dress, the things they do, and the way they live, and since most old photographs have some people on them, that alone makes them worth studying.

After last year's book, I had letters from expatriate Sheffielders in Australia, Canada, the United States, Scotland and Southern England, most of whom had been sent the book as a Christmas present from relatives still living in the city, and most of whom seemed to enjoy the memories it revived. I also had a large number of letters and telephone calls from people nearer home wanting to give me more information about the pictures I used, or just wanting to chat about one picture or another. It was all very entertaining and often very informative.

Once again, most of the pictures used in this book are from my own collection of old picture postcards. Where they are not, I have made it clear in the captions.

T his is the Mark 2 version of Peter Harvey's Sheffield, another selection of photographs showing how Sheffield used to look before traffic cluttered the streets. On the other side of the coin, it is also the Sheffield in which housewives battled against persistent grime, donkey-stoned their front steps, black-leaded their firegrates, and ponched their washing.

First published in 1981 by Sheaf Publishing,
85 Mooroaks Road, Sheffield S10 1BX
Printed by South Yorkshire Printers Ltd
Text copyright: Peter Harvey
Design copyright: Sheaf Publishing
SBN 0 9505458 6 4

Spot the differences in these two views of
Fargate, one taken about thirty years after the
other.

On the early picture, the overhead tram-
lines are carried on poles down the centre of
the street, between the tram tracks; there is no
Kemsley House; the street is gas lit from small
gas lamps; the tram car has no top; and there
isn't a motor vehicle in sight.

The sign on one of the buildings on the
right hand side is advertising Bonnet and Sons
Famous Chocolates ('made daily on the

premises'), and the shop on the left is that of
Harold W. Mills and Co, furnishing ironmongers.

On the later picture, the little gas lamps
have gone, the tram poles have been moved,
Kemsley House has been built, and there are
motor cars, although not nearly as many as
there were to be later.

(One of the trams, by the way, is No. 202,
which, in 1935 and early 1936, appeared in an
experimental all light blue livery, as it appears
here, which gives some clue as to when the
photograph was taken).

I always had a liking for the little rock garden
which can be seen here sandwiched between
two trams. It stood roughly where the Goodwin
Fountain is now. There was a small pool in it
and a trickle of water which had worn smooth
some of the white stones. Of all the features
which have been placed at this point, the
obelisk, Queen Victoria's statue, and even the
present fountain, I think the rock garden was
probably the most attractive.

4

Town Hall Square, 1897

The earliest of all Sheffield picture postcards are those issued to mark the visit of Queen Victoria in 1897, when she performed the official opening of the Town Hall.

Although plain postcards, without illustration, were introduced in this country on 1st October, 1870, it was not until the late 1890's that picture cards were introduced, and today, pre-1900 cards are very hard to find.

Sheffield togged itself up no end for the Queen's arrival on 21st May 1897. Being very fond of erecting huge mock arches at that time, they built arches over as many streets as possible, draped bunting and strings of flags over anything that was drapable, and erected what looked like a large open-sided marquee at the bottom of Barkers Pool.

The Queen arrived at the Midland Station, processed in an open carriage to the Town Hall with an escort of 127 officers and men from the Life Guards. Waiting for her at Pinstone Street were a guard of honour from the Hallamshire Battalion of the York and Lancaster Regiment and a gathering of civic dignitaries.

After opening the building the royal party processed to Norfolk Park where about 50,000 children were gathered to welcome her, then she went down to the east end to look at Cammell and Co's Cyclops Works.

The entire visit, three ceremonies and a six-mile journey through city streets in a carriage, took only two hours. During it, she gave the Master Cutler a baronetcy and the deputy mayor a knighthood, and a few days later she conferred the title of Lord Mayor, instead of Mayor, on the city's chief citizen.

Pinstone Street, 1897

Barkers Pool, 1897

GIRLS GATHERING RASPBERRIES AT THE — — ENGLISH FRUIT PRESERVING Cº⁵ FARM, STOCKSBRIDGE. — AUG 1904 —

"ENCOURAGE HOME INDUSTRIES"

In my blissful ignorance, I never thought of the Sheffield region as a fruit-growing area so when I first saw this card I thought it must be a photograph taken at Stocksbridge, Norfolk, or Stocksbridge, Somerset. But it isn't. It was taken at Stocksbridge, South Yorkshire.

On looking into it, I found that a Mr. Oxley, who apparently came from Hillsborough, set up the English Fruit Preserving Company farm at Stocksbridge where fruit was grown and made into jam. The enterprise was very successful and became well known in the district where it was colloquially referred to as 'Jammy's Fruit Farm'.

During the gathering season it was very popular with the local girls and women who became temporary fruit pickers.

Mr. Oxley eventually gave the land to the local authority on condition that a park was set up.

HMS Beresford sailed through the streets of Sheffield during the 1910 General Election campaigns - there were two, one in January, the other in December - in support of the Conservative cause, the message being that the Conservatives would build up the Royal Navy, thereby making the country safe and providing work for Sheffield.

In the January election, Asquith and the Liberals stayed in power although they lost one hundred seats, and they kept power by a very narrow margin in the December election.

The Beresford after whom this peculiar craft was named was Admiral Lord Charles Beresford, sailor (with a long list of commands) and politician (with a reputation for speaking at every opportunity, sometimes aggressively, on naval matters).

I'm not quite sure of the mechanics of HMS Beresford. Presumably it was either towed along on wheels or it was mounted on some kind of vehicle.

OUR NAVY MUST BE SUPREME

H.M.S. BERESFORD

WE WANT WORK! NOT PROMISES

PRINTED & PUBLISHED BY WOOLLEN & CO., LTD • YORK STREET, SHEFFIELD.

The Radicals are Starving our **NAVY**, and if allowed to continue will leave us an easy victim for Foreign Foes. Prevent this at all costs by **VOTING BLUE**. **A STRONG NAVY** and **WORK FOR SHEFFIELD MEN.**

Canvassing votes, 1910

Between 1916 and 1918, Cammell Lairds, the Sheffield steel firm, issued a set of coloured art postcards showing scenes inside a steelworks. Because it was war-time, the designs had to be approved by the censor before they could be published, and I believe that altogether there were twenty different designs, several of them signed by an artist called E. F. Skinner.

Because so many of them show men working with red hot, or white hot, metal, the designs tend to be quite dramatic and the artwork is very effective.

One of the best known of these cards showed women shell workers. An oil painting of this design titled For King and Country,

was presented to Queen Mary when she and King George V visited the Cammell Laird works in May 1919. The pictures were also used in several brochures produced by the firm.

Shell Workers at Cammell Laird

Ecclesfield Hospital Parade, 1908

If there was one thing Edwardian Sheffielders knew how to do, it was how to let themselves go in a worthy cause.

Give them a gala, or a parade, or best of all a parade which ended in a gala, and if the cause was a good one they would black their faces, dress up in outlandish clothes, and transform ordinary tradesmen's drays into a riot of colour.

The group of gentlemen seen here with a fine variety of headgear and facial adornments, were taking part in the Ecclesfield Hospital Parade of 1908. Judging from the fact that nearly every one of them seems to be carrying a musical instrument of some kind, it's a fair guess that they were the band. The euphonium player has entered the spirit of the occasion magnificently. He has an advertisement for Brasso metal polish where he usually carries his music.

The dray to the right, decorated in aid of Sheffield Medical Charities, has an industrial theme. The old Sheffield grinder sits at his wheel, smoking his pipe, behind him three youngsters who have come along for the ride.

It's marvellous what could be done with an empty coal cart, a bit of imagination and several thousand flowers.

The lower dray is the effort of St. Wilfrid's Church, in this case, I believe, for a Band of Hope gala. Again, there is a wealth of flowers, but there seems also to have been an attempt to get into the Edwardian equivalent of the Guinness Book of Records for the largest number of children on one dray. It's hard to see how they could have got any more on there. Anyway, they make a fine turnout.

St. Wilfrid's Church dray

Mr. Ernest Blenkinsop

Ernest Blenkinsop captained Sheffield Wednesday and England, made nearly four hundred appearances for Wednesday, led them to two First Division championships, in 1928-29 and 1929-30, won twenty-six international caps - a record for a Sheffield player at that time - and was one of the best full backs in the game.

Born at Cudworth, he played for Hull City before joining Wednesday. He went to Liverpool in 1934, but when his playing days finished there, returned to Sheffield and in later years was licensee of the Sportsman's Inn, Crosspool. He died in 1969, but even today remains one of those players of whom older Wednesday-ites talk in awed tones.

He appears here, in his England shirt, because having used a picture of Ernest Needham, of Sheffield United, last year, I feel obliged to keep the balance and avoid upsetting my friends of the other persuasion.

Nowadays the FA Cup rarely comes to Sheffield except - as it did recently - when it is in need of running repairs. Sheffield teams do not win it as often as they did in the old days.

After nearly forty-six cup-less years, it is comforting to recall that the last time it was here for a full year, when Sheffield Wednesday won it in 1935, at least we made good use of it.

It was placed on display at Cole Brothers store for a week and cards like this one were sold at twopence each to raise money for King George's Jubilee Trust.

King George V, that is. Goodness knows who will be on the throne by the time a Sheffield team wins it again.

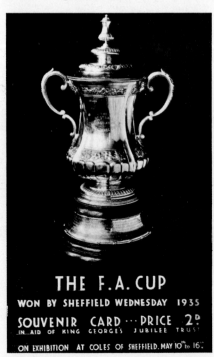

F.A. Cup

W. Edward Platts signature

Mr. Ernest Harper

Edward Platts, sometimes apparently own as William, sometimes as 'Gus', was of the pioneer speedway riders in Sheffield n 1929, when the first meeting at Owlerton attended by 15,000 people, till 1933, when sport hit hard times and the track was ed for five years.

Unfortunately, it is the only picture I have Sheffield speedway star. I would like to some of the others because it has always med to me that they had such colourful nes - Scotty Cumming, Clem 'Daredevil' kett, Smoky Spencer Stratton, Bronco Dixon, Dusty Haigh, for example.

The athletic gentleman - and by all accounts t is exactly what he was, a quiet, modest rtsman and gentleman - is the greatest long ance runner Sheffield ever produced, est Harper.

He started his running career in 1921 when he entered the Stannington Steeplechase and won it. From then on he won scores of trophies, ran for England many times, and took part in three Olympic Games, Paris in 1924, Amsterdam in 1928, and Berlin in 1936, when he won the silver medal in the marathon.

Harper returned nome to Sheffield to a hero's welcome and a public subscription raised enough money to buy him a house at Stannington where he lived till 1958 when he and his wife emigrated to Australia to join their daughter. He died in Australia at the age of 77 in 1979.

The Village.

G. Sprigg
Handsworth.

The Cross Keys, Handsworth

The Cross Keys, Handsworth, seen here at a time when Retford Road was little more than a lane, is said to be the only public house in Britain situated in a churchyard. The churchyard belongs to St. Mary's Church and is indeed behind, and to the side of, the pub.

This comes about because in olden days the building used to be the church house. It was used as a school from 1600 to 1800 when it was sold to the parish clerk for £43. Later it became a public house.

There has always been a story that a secret tunnel runs from the cellar of the house out towards where Handsworth Hall used to be and that this was an escape route in days of yore so that the priest could get away if ever the ungodly arrived intent on doing him mischief.

During the 1930's a tunnel hewn out of solid rock was discovered during nearby roadworks and it looked at first as though this was the tunnel of the story. Then some spoilsport engineer came along and said the tunnel was too modern to be an old escape route, and anyway it didn't go anywhere, and he thought it was simply a bit of extra storage space somebody had dug out for the pub at some time which had, for some reason, been bricked up later.

The romantics among us don't set too much store by what spoilsport engineers say. We still believe in a secret tunnel and if that wasn't it, then it is somewhere else.

The Whirlow Bridge Inn was demolished in 1938 for road widening, but by then had not been a pub for some years. It had been converted into cottages.

William Hutchinson Brougham, whose name appears so prominently above the doorway of the Peacock Hotel, was quite well known in Sheffield. In his younger days he managed a hay and straw dealers' business in Pond Street, then he became proprietor of the Punch Bowl on The Moor, and later he moved to the Peacock where he stayed for 15 years till his death in April 1903.

New Inn, Hemsworth

SALT BOX, PSALTER LANE SHEFFIELD

Salt Box Cottages, Psalter Lane

These cottages, known as the Saltbox Cottages, used to stand near the crest of the hill at Psalter Lane. According to one account I have read, they got their name because of their peculiar shape which made them look like a saltbox hanging from a kitchen wall. Not knowing what a saltbox looks like, I find it hard to judge. Anyway, whatever the accuracy of their name, the cottages were a well known landmark on Psalter Lane for many years.

The reason they are perched up above the level of the road is that some time in the mid-1800's Psalter Lane was lowered by about four feet at this point to make it less steep. The footpath, and the houses, are on the original road level. When the road was lowered, a safety wall was built along the edge of the pavement.

The backs of the cottages were built on to solid rock, so there was only one entrance to each cottage, at the front.

The houses described as the oldest in Sheffield were on Commonside. It was said that the date 1758 was engraved above the mantelpiece of one of them. They were included in a Corporation clearance order in the late 1930s, but it was some years later before they were demolished.

According to the caption, the dwelling on the far right is the Keeper's Cottage at Ryecroft Glen, Dore. The keeper was evidently partial to ivy. In fact, the word that springs to mind is verdant.

There is so much greenery on and around this little house that you wouldn't think it was Sheffield at all, you'd think it was some little spot in the New Forest.

At the other extreme of the verdure scale, and unmistakeably in Sheffield, Brook Cottages belong to a time when there were still people living at Attercliffe. These days the area looks like a corner of the Sahara that's been used for the dumping of builder's rubble.

Commonside

Keeper's Cottage, Ryecroft Glen

16

In last year's book I included (on page 7) a picture of an event which was a mystery to me. It did not remain a mystery for long. Within hours of the book being published I received a telephone call from a gentleman telling me he was certain it was a photograph of the stone-laying ceremony at the Victoria Hall.

Since then I have had telephone calls or letters from about fifty people, of whom about forty-eight agreed with the Victoria Hall theory, and the other two thought the event photographed might have something to do with the Cathedral (because the building in the background had a sign on it saying Cole Brothers).

It certainly was a picture of an event on the site of what is now the Victoria Hall. Of that I am certain. The building in the background is the old furniture repository that Cole Brothers used to have on Norfolk Street.

But although at first I went along with the idea that it was taken at the stone-laying ceremony, now I'm not so sure. The stone-laying took place in late September, 1906, but a notice on the picture I used last year (a notice obviously erected specially for the event), is advertising the June number of a magazine called the Home Messenger. I don't think they would have been advertising the June issue of a magazine at the stone-laying in September.

Anyway, whatever the actual event was, it was connected with the building of the Victoria Hall.

In view of the interest aroused by this photograph, I thought it might be worthwhile using another mystery picture this year, so here it is.

There's even less to go on this time. It looks suspiciously like another stone-laying, but of what building, and where?

Unfortunately, the principal people on the picture, the ones with the top hats on, who are the most likely to be recognized, have their backs to the camera. There are no helpful signs anywhere. But there is just a chance that somebody might recognize the houses in the background, or one of the spectators.

At a wild guess, based on very little, I'd say it was at Woodseats.

There used to be a good many farms in and around Sheffield but they disappeared as the city grew outwards. Woodend Farm on the opposite page was at Millhouses. It stood on land now taken up by factories at Archer Road, and the Midland Railway line can be seen in the background on the right of the picture.

Woodend Farm, Millhouses. M&S 796.

Woodend Farm, Millhouses

Baron Street, off Clough Road

These four views, of Totley Rise, Newlyn Road, Woodseats, Sheldon Road, and Baron Street, near Bramall Lane football ground, all have something in common. Every one has a cross written on it somewhere. 'X' marks the spot.

Old time postcard senders were very fond of putting crosses on their postcards. Sometimes the cross is explained on the back of the card in the written message. Often it is not. Explained or not, what it usually meant was this is where I live, or this is where we are staying, or this is aunty's house, or something similar.

In this respect, old time postcard senders had an advantage over us because in their day there were postcards showing almost every street. Nowadays, the only cards on sale show views of the city centre. There are no views of suburban streets for people to indicate their homes.

I even came across one old card on which a young man, writing to his lady friend, had marked a cross on the window of the bedroom in which he was sitting writing the card. That really is pinpoint accuracy.

The odd thing about the picture of Sheldon Road is how half-dressed it looks without the trees that now line it. From their size I had always assumed that the trees had been planted when the road was built. Obviously not.

Sheldon Road, Nether Edge

It's difficult to imagine now, but the Broomhall area used to be a select private estate known as Broom Hall Park. To discourage unwanted traffic, there were gates across the roads leading into the estate, in Broomhall Road, Park Lane, and at the top and bottom of Collegiate Crescent.

From this picture of one of the old gates, they were pretty sturdy obstacles too, not the sort of thing you would want to run your horse and trap into on a dark night.

The gates were eventually removed in 1916 and the roads in the estate were then dedicated so that traffic could move freely through them.

Broomhall Place, pictured at about the same time, has a sedate, upstairs-downstairs look about it.

Park Lane, Broomhall

DCLIFFE HALL, SHEFFIELD.

At the other end of the housing scale, and some very well kept shrubbery igloos, and a stately wheelbarrow, Endcliffe Hall looks most distinguished.

It was built, in forty acres of grounds, in the 1860's by Sir John Brown, the famous Sheffield industrialist, and it was his home for some years. In 1893, the Endcliffe Hall Estate was offered to Sheffield Corporation for £70,000, which was said at the time to be about half of what it had cost to build, but the Corporation decided not to buy, and in 1916, the mansion was bought for the Territorial Army and has remained in military use ever since.

In these days when a modestly-sized semi can cost upwards of £30,000, it's an odd thought that it would once have been possible to buy a place like this for £70,000.

Still, even if I bought something this big, I'd never be able to afford curtains and carpets.

THE TINSLEY PARK COLLIER...

WORKING PLACE IN BARNSLEY SEA...

When the craze for collecting picture postcards was at its height, between 1900 and 1914, firms and businesses caught on to the fact that here was a cheap and useful advertising medium.

The chocolate firms - particularly Fry's and Faulder's - soap makers, biscuit makers, friendly societies, railway companies, shipping companies, boot and shoe manufacturers, and many more issued advertising postcards which were sometimes sent out with their products, and often used for correspondence with customers.

In Sheffield, as elsewhere, postcards were used for advertising. The card for the Tinsley Park Colliery Company Ltd., shows a little bit of Sheffield that not many people ever saw - a short stretch of the Barnsley seam, from which came the best household coal for miles around.

The height of the tunnel here was four-feet-six inches from floor to ceiling.

Tinsley Park Colliery is long gone. There isn't even a trace of where it used to be. What with the building of the Parkway to Catcliffe, and extensive opencast operations, the land scape in that part of Sheffield has changed beyond recognition.

he advertising card of the lorry here was issued by
mes Farrer and Sons Ltd., of Devonshire Works,
vision Street. They made buff wheels, glazers, bobs,
ops, dolleys, compos, machines, and supplied polishing
ne, emery wheels, buffing sand etc. Since much of
is information is painted on the side of the lorry,
nat better illustration for an advertisement than the
ry itself, stacked up with a selection of the said goods?

It wasn't only the big firms who used cards as
verts. The picture of the lady in the ankle-length
stume, all dressed up and ready for action, is advert-
ng a ladies' tailors in St. Philip's Road.

The little silhouette is one of a charming set of
rds, all done in silhouette, published to advertise
adsley Flower Show. They are signed by H. J. Leslie,
d whoever Mr. or Ms. Leslie was, he or she had a nice
uch. Wadsley Flower Show, incidentally, was quite an
portant event in its day.

My thanks to Mr. Kenneth Dibnah for allowing me
borrow the James Farrer lorry card.

DEVONSHIRE WORKS, SHEFFIELD.

Mr. & Mrs. ALBERT ELING,
Ladies' Tailors and Costumiers,
275, St. Philip's Road, Sheffield.

Advertising Cards

...Puts on deerstalker hat, lights large meerschaum pipe, and tried hard to look like Basil Ràthbone...

This photograph bristles with clues, so that with close study, a certain amount of research and a spot of Holmesian deduction, it is possible to work out when the picture was taken, almost to the day.

On the left is an electric, covered-top tram car so the picture was obviously taken after 1899, when the first electric tram car ran, and after March 1903, when the first covered-top tram was introduced. In the centre is a statue of Queen Victoria which used to stand in Town Hall Square, so the picture was taken after May 1905, when the statue was unveiled. Also in the centre is the Cinema House thus proving that the picture was taken after May 1913, when the Cinema House opened.

So much for the afters. Now for the befores.

There is no sign of the City Hall so the picture was taken before 1933 when the City Hall opened and before 1931 when Queen Victoria's statue was bundled off to Endcliffe Park. It was probably taken before 1929 because that was the year that the City Hall foundation stone was laid and there is no sign on the photograph of any work on the site at all. In fact the old property is still there.

Now it gets slightly more complicated.

With a magnifying glass it is possible to see that the tram is number 369 and the reference books say that number 369 was not introduced into service till 1921. Now we have narrowed the picture to a decade. It was taken some time between 1921 and 1929.

Now it gets even more complicated.

The billboard outside the Cinema House is advertising two films called 'Darlin'' and 'The Fourteenth Lover'. Reference to the film record books shows that these two films did the rounds in this country in 1923.

It is obvious that the picture was taken in warmish weather, since nobody is wearing an overcoat, so a quick scamper through the files of the Sheffield Daily Telegraph for the summer months of 1923 is called for. This proves that 'Darlin'', starring Colleen Moore, was on at the Cinema House from Monday, 16th July to Wednesday, 18th July, 1923, and 'The Fourteenth Lover' starring Viola Dana, was on for the rest of the week, Thursday 19th July to Saturday 21st July.

Now it gets incredibly complicated.

From the position of the shadow made by the Town Hall tower, the photograph was taken at about ten o'clock or eleven o'clock in the morning. It is too busy for a Sunday morning and not busy enough for Saturday. It could not have been the Monday or Thursday mornings because, according to that week's weather reports, it rained both mornings. I doubt if it was taken on the Friday because the weather reports say that Friday was a windless day and there is a stiffish breeze blowing the coat of the lady on the right of the picture.

There was a fresh westerly wind blowing on the Tuesday and Wednesday. There we have it. The photograph was taken on the morning of Tuesday 17th July, or Wednesday 18th July, 1923. Over on the other side of the road from the Town Hall there is a man carring a newspaper. Unfortunately, I cannot make out the date on the front page.

...Takes off deerstalker hat, douses meerschaum pipe, and collapses in exhausted heap on nearby chaise longue...

Town Hall Square

PIANOS WILSON PECK Ld PIANOS &
BEETHOVEN HOUSE.
CINEMA HOUSE
THE FOURTEENTH LOVER
WILSON PECK

Lowfield C.l. School. Empire Day. 1907 M&S.

Lowfield Council School, 1907

There are quite a number of old postcards showing pictures of Sheffield schools but not many have children on them, and schools are fairly dull places without children.

The boys of Lowfield Council School, all temporarily on the knee, are not about to set off in an unusual handicap race, they are in training for the Empire Day Pageant of 1907, when thousands of children assembled at Bramall Lane and, among other things, formed the words of appropriate messages and slogans. Lowfield were obviously responsible for the letter M. The rest of the message was presumably being practised at other schools.

Wadsley National School has four boys leaning over the school wall in a fairly typical schoolboy pose, unlike Birley Carr school, built 1905, and described on the caption as being 'new'.

Judging from the young ladies' hats and scarves, the leafless bush, the muddy boots and the exceptionally large number of hands stuffed deep into pockets, this early shot of Norton School was taken on a cold winter's day. In fact, there seems to be a bit of left-over snow in the foreground.

As one who lived in that part of the city for some time I can confirm that Norton and the top end of Gleadless Valley are areas where snow lingers for days - and sometimes weeks - after it has disappeared from the more temperate zones such as Heeley and Sharrow. It is, as they say in Sheffield, a top coat colder up at Norton.

This probably accounts for the hardy footwear worn by most of the young gentlemen here.

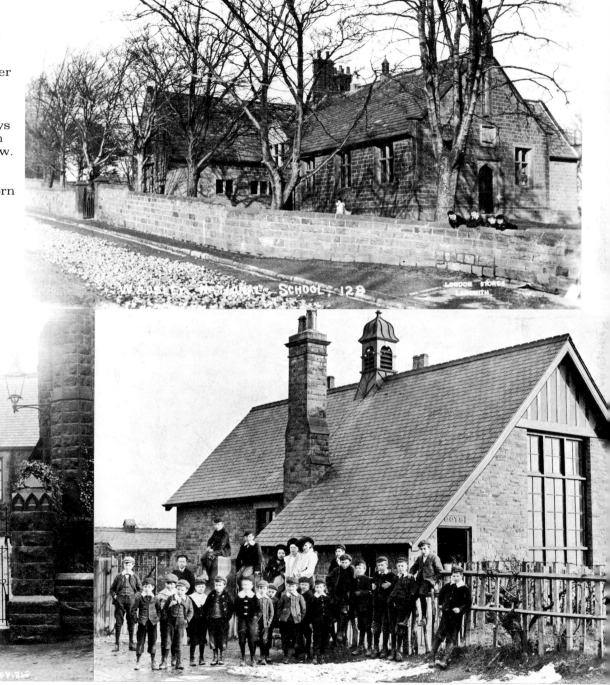

Birley Carr School

Norton School

The man who took the photograph on the left captioned it simply 'Daisies, Hillsborough Park', and in a way there is nothing remarkable about it at all. It is just an old lady chaperoning four young children as they pick daisies, nothing more.

But I like it. I like the earnest young faces staring intently at the camera, the hands clutching small bunches of flowers, the lady with a newspaper folded neatly on her knee, a parasol by her side. I like the air of warm tranquility it has.

The daisy season was long past by the time the decorated arch in Oakes Park, Norton, was photographed. Most of the triumphal arches erected in the Sheffield area in the early days were for visiting royalty. But not this one.

Miss Bagshawe, eldest daughter of the late Mr. F. W. Bagshawe, of Oakes Park, was married in November 1907, to Mr. Henry Bradshaw-Isherwood, of Marple Hall, Cheshire.

When the couple returned from their honeymoon, on 23rd December, festivities were organised to welcome them home by a combined committee made up of tenants and members of Norton Ploughing Association.

Arches decorated with fairy lights and the words 'Welcome Home' and 'Norton Greets You' were built in the village, and in the park itself this arch was built over the drive to the house saying 'Health and Happiness'.

Whit sings were always a big event in Sheffield. Everybody turned out in their best, the Sunday School banners were unfurled, the programmes printed and the floral decorations spruced up.

Usually, there was a photographer on hand to make sure the event was duly recorded.

This particular Whit sing was at High Hazels Park, Darnall. Among the banners on show are Woodbourn Road Wesleyan Reform Church, Attercliffe Wesleyan Methodist Sunday School, and the Ebenezer Baptists.

By any standards it's a very appealing picture with lots of atmosphere about it. But for me it has a very special significance. The smiling teenage girl just to the side of the lady with a handkerchief to her mouth, peeking round another lady's hat, is my mum.

Oakes Park

High Hazels Park

It is a long time since I sat at Wyming Brook on a hot summer day with my feet dangling in the water, anticipating the imminent pleasure of seeing off a satchel full of sandwiches and a bottle of Tizer, but I can remember it well.

Wyming Brook, a picturesque ravine in 210 acres of land which was bought by the Corporation in 1906 and opened up by the building of Wyming Brook Drive in 1908-9, is a lovely place to be on a hot day.

It was very popular among photographers in the two or three years after it was opened to the public. Unlike most photographers, the man who took this picture managed to get some people into his shot. There are four of them, unless, of course, there are any more of them hiding in the bushes.

Assuming that the photographer has not arranged them this way specially for artistic effect, they appear to me to be somewhat oddly juxtaposed. Why, for instance, is the young lady with the enigmatic smile on the left, sitting on the opposite river bank from the others? Why does the gentleman with the beard look as if he is clenching his fist at the photographer? Is he perhaps indicating that if the photographer doesn't make off immediately and take his contraption with him, trouble will ensue? Is that a sewing machine the lady on the right has her hand on? If so, why? And are they not all looking a mite sheepish?

We shall never know. The lady on the left has a full basket which no doubt contains their lunch, so it is perhaps best that we stop asking impertinent questions and leave them to their al fresco meal.

The ladies in the photograph below have chosen to spend their Sunday in a more sedentary fashion, and they offer an answer to anybody who ever wondered how it came about that there were so many paintings of Beauchief Abbey bobbing about the oceans of the art world.

The abbey is in the process of being painted in triplicate, or possibly in quadruplicate if the young lady on the left is painting without an easel and not just giving moral support to her friend.

There is another possibility, of course. It could be the annual shindig of the Sheffield and District Lady Artists Society. There may be another twenty or thirty of them busily painting away just off the picture.

Beauchief Abbey

Wyming Brook

As an antidote to the impression that is often given that the Edwardian years were one long, peaceful summer, without so much as a mild ground frost to upset things, this is a picture of how deep the snow was near Fox House one year.

Assuming that the two gentlemen are about five feet nine or ten, the snow looks to be about six and a half feet deep, which is a heavy fall even by the standards of Oberjoch or Garmisch-Partenkirchen.

And they didn't have gritters in those days.

It was probably the same year that the fountain that used to stand outside Weston Park Museum froze over, giving it a slightly novel wedding-cake appearance and causing the local photographers to rush up to take a picture. There are at least three different postcards of the frozen fountain.

Fountain, Weston Park

Snow Drift Nr Fox House Where the Mail had to be dug out

J W M

The Bleriot monoplane standing on the grass at Redmires with a crowd around it is a picture I have seen used in one old newspaper in which it was described as a photograph of the first aeroplane to land in Sheffield. This it was not.

The date is Saturday 3rd August 1912 and the pilot of the plane is a chap called Robert Slack, who was a student at the International Correspondence School. Mr. Slack undertook to do a 1,100-mile flight around the country to publicise the school, and it can be seen on the picture that the aircraft has the letters I.C.S. on each wing.

Poor Mr. Slack had a bit of a rough ride to reach Sheffield. It took him eleven hours to get here from Harrogate. Not all that time was spent flying. He was forced to put down twice because of thick fog and bouts of airsickness.

At Redmires, where a crowd had gathered to greet him, white sheets were placed on the ground to help him find the landing area. Once down, he had to stay for a week. Bad weather delayed his take-off for Rugby.

Later the same month Gustav Hamel flew to Sheffield from Buxton and stayed for three days, and in November 1912, J. L. Hall, the Sheffield aviator, gave exhibition flights at Redmires for a week.

But the first record I have been able to find of an aeroplane landing in Sheffield is in July 1911, when S. F. Cody landed at Tinsley. He didn't mean to land there. He was taking part in a race around Britain at the time and was forced down by an emergency. And he only stayed for half an hour. But strictly speaking, intentional or not, he was the first.

Things could have been quite different, however, for it is not widely realised that one of the pioneers of aviation was an Attercliffe lad.

John Stringfellow was born at Attercliffe on 6th December 1799 and grew up there. When he was old enough to work he was apprenticed to the lace trade at Nottingham, and unfortunately that is where his link with Sheffield ends. He later became a bobbin and carriage manufacturer, and about 1820 moved to Chard, Somerset.

There he met Samuel Henson, an engineer and, since both of them were interested in the possibility of flying machines, they formed the Aerial Steam Transit Company and started making models. In 1847, they made a large model with twenty-feet long wings. They had great hopes for it, but when they launched the model, it failed to fly, and Henson, discouraged, emigrated soon afterwards to America.

Stringfellow, being an Attercliffe lad, kept trying. In 1848 he completed a model measuring ten feet from wing tip to wing tip and powered by a steam engine. Tested at Chard, it rose from the ground and flew for thirty feet. This is said to be the first time in the history of the world that any aircraft made free powered flight. He took his machine to London where it went on exhibition, and in another test, flew for forty yards. For some reason he seems to have lost interest in the possibility of flying machines at this point.

Twenty years later he was invited by the Aeronautical Society to compete in an exhibition at the Crystal Palace and he took a steam driven model which flew along a wire. For this, the society awarded him one hundred pounds.

He died in December 1883 at Chard where there is a memorial to him as 'the inventor of the first engine-driven aeroplane to fly'.

If only he had kept going with his experiments after that first great success he might have beaten the Wright Brothers to it.

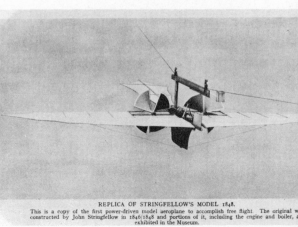

REPLICA OF STRINGFELLOW'S MODEL 1848.
This is a copy of the first power-driven model aeroplane to accomplish free flight. The original was constructed by John Stringfellow in 1846/1848 and portions of it, including the engine and boiler, are exhibited in the Museum.

Replica of Mr. Stringfellow's Flying Machine, 1848

For the more discerning traveller, who planned his journey with a Bradshaw and valued the comfort of horsehair-filled cushions and anti-macassars, the railway was more becoming.

At Sheffield's Midland Station the time approaches ten-thirty and one of the Midland Railway's stately little 2-4-0's, No. 266, stands on platform two with what looks like a single clerestory-roof coach. The engine driver takes the opportunity to exchange a few pleasantries with an otherwise-unoccupied porter, and there is a singular absence of passengers.

Over on platform one, an itinerant railway policeman and half a dozen people who might be potential passengers, show a keen interest in what the photographer is doing and the station bookstall seems to be going through one of its slack periods.

Apart from the locomotive, and the dress of the people, the station hasn't changed a great deal.

It always seemed to me when I was young that Eccles[
tram terminus was way out in the country, halfway tc
Manchester.

Tram terminii, wherever they were, tended to insp
a certain amount of panic as you walked towards then
From 800 yards you saw there was a tram in, and
quickened your pace. From 600 yards, if the tram was
still in, you quickened even more. From 400 yards it
always looked as though the driver was getting up frc
his rest and stretching, which is what they always dic
just before they set off back to town, so you started tc
trot. The last 100 yards were completed at the gallop.

Then you sat there puffing and panting for ten
minutes waiting for the tram to set off.

Nether Green tram terminus, Fulwood Road

One of the noticeable things about last year's book was the number of people who contacted me to say that they had recognized a friend or relative on one of the pictures.

Since all those who spoke to me regarded it as a pleasant surprise to turn the page of a book and suddenly see Uncle Ernest or Aunt Dora staring out at them, I have included another set of groups.

Tram conductresses (or female tram conductors, as they were called) were introduced on Sheffield trams in June 1915. By the time this picture was taken in 1918 (the photographer's caption says it was 1819, but this is what we in newspapers call a slight boob), they were well established, and looking very smart too.

This card was loaned to me by a friend of mine, Mrs. Betty Oades, and I'm most grateful to her because I think it is a lovely picture.

The group of musicians is the Sheffield Comrades Military Band, and they must have been competent because they won the Crossfield Challenge Cup in a competition at Blackpool in 1920. I daresay they worked up a healthy thirst doing it too.

Sheffield Comrades' Military Band

The young sportsmen are members of the Burgoyne Road Boys' Football and Swimming Club, and if the Sheffield Elementary Schools Shield and the medals they are all wearing are anything to go by, they were a pretty good outfit. The date of this one is 1907.

I don't know a great deal about the Salvation Army Band, except that I am informed by a friend who is in the Salvation Army that No. 2 Band used to be based at Harvest Lane.

Sheffield No. 2 Band, Salvation Army

H. Coward Esq., Mus. Doc. Oxon.

The Sheffield Choir was a world-famous organisation in its day. In 1911, the 200-strong choir, known as the Sheffield Musical Union Chorus, did a six-month tour of the world giving 134 concerts in Canada, the United States, Honolulu, Fiji, Australia, New Zealand and South Africa. During the tour, more than three quarters of a million people attended their concerts.

The moving force behind all this success was the choirmaster, Dr. Henry Coward, who later became Sir Henry Coward.

Dr. Coward, who was born at Liverpool, started work at the age of eight in Sheffield, with no thoughts of taking up music. At the age of twenty-two, he left business and became a teacher and it was not until he was thirty-nine that he became a professional musician. At fifty he was made a Doctor of Music at Oxford University, and from then on, although he taught, composed and wrote books, it was as the master chorus master that he achieved fame.

This picture of the choir is an early example of flashlight photography.

Norfolk Picture Palace, Duke Street

Coliseum, Heeley

Oxford, Upperthorpe

Manor Cinema, Manor Top

In any group of people over the age of thirty nothing turns on the hot tap of nostalgia quite so freely as the subject of old cinemas. Mere mention of the Forum, the Chantrey, the Paragon, the Sunbeam, the Globe, the Ritz, the Roscoe, the Roxy, or any one of about forty others, is enough to flood a room the size of the Cutlers' Hall with fond recollections.

This affection for the old suburban cinemas is not altogether surprising because they were not just buildings where films were shown.

They were places where the patrons did all manner of things. (Even in the most humble, moth-eaten, 150-seat cinema you were always a patron, not just a customer). At the pictures, people met friends and neighbours, caught up with the news, celebrated, courted, and occasionally nodded off.

They dropped bits of choc-ice on their clothes as they watched the screen instead of what they were eating, hunted anxiously through newly-opened packets of potato crisps for the bit of blue paper containing the salt, and perfected the art of unwrapping a toffee in the shortest possible time with the minimum amount of noise.

Before going in, they sometimes had a drink at the nearby herbalists' shop. On going in they said good evening to the manager, and after coming out they often had a bag of chips on the way home.

Going to the pictures was a complete experience.

The giant enigma of all this is how, since everybody apparently loved them to distraction, it came about that the suburban cinemas eventually had so few patrons they had to convert to bingo or close. At the time of writing, only the Rex, Intake, survives. The others have all gone, but their former patrons continue to talk about them.

I have to confess that I am as guilty as anyone in this respect. My locals were the Plaza, Handsworth, Darnall Cinema, the Lyric and the Balfour, also at Darnall, and the Regal, Attercliffe, with occasional expeditions to the Rex, the Abbeydale, and the Scala.

At the slightest excuse I can reminisce about them at great length and to the unutterable boredom of anybody who grew up elsewhere and has his own memories about cinemas in his own neck of the woods.

Picture postcards showing close-ups of suburban cinemas are very hard to find. These four pictures, of Heeley Coliseum, the Manor at Manor Top, the Norfolk on Duke Street, and the Oxford, Upperthorpe, are not postcards. They are from the files of Sheffield Newspapers Ltd., to whom I am grateful for permitting me to use them.

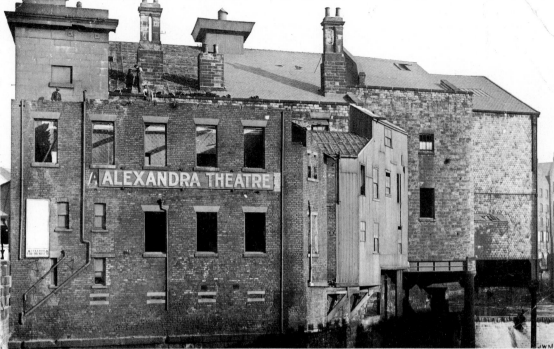

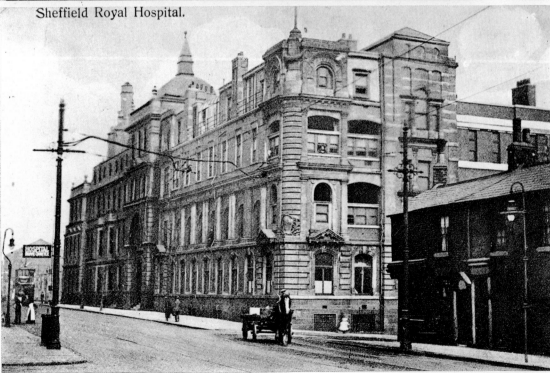

Sheffield Royal Hospital.

Royal Hospital, West Street

The old Alexandra Theatre in Blonk Street closed after the last performance of The Bonnie Pit Lad on 28th March 1914. The demolition men moved in quickly and by 20th May the building had gone and Sheffield had lost yet another of its old theatres.

This picture was taken soon after the closure. The windows have been removed, the inside gutted, half the slates have gone and four of the demolition men can be seen working on the roof.

The billboard is still in place though, advertising the old Alex as 'The home of drama. Twice nightly. 6.50 and 9'.

Postcard publishers do not sell this kind of picture any more. They publish plenty of pretty town centre pictures, with flowers and trees and blazing sunshine, but they no longer attempt to show changes as they take place.

The Royal Hospital, for example, which has been demolished within the last twelve months, was not shown on a postcard in the process of being knocked down. Western Bank, Brook Hill and Leavygreave, seen here as they used to look, have undergone enormous changes, but once again, the changes went unrecorded by the people who sell picture postcards.

The postcard collectors of the future will have very little to show them what happened in Sheffield during the 1970's and 1080's.

Sheffield from the University 190

Melbourne Avenu

Whitham Rd. JWM.

Gas lamp, Mooroaks Road

Whitham Roa

Delivery boys were once a common sight, and here we see three of them plying their trade.

The boy on the pavement edge at Whitham Road is wearing the standard delivery boy's apron but carries what looks suspiciously like an empty wooden beer crate. Perhaps he has just completed his round from the local beer-off.

The boy in the snow at Crookes has a more conventional basket and is demonstrating the art of carrying it. When loaded to the brim with muffins, tea-cakes, Sally Lunns or whatever, the delivery boy had to lean away from his basket to counterbalance its weight. This gave him a pronounced list to port or starboard, depending on which hip he rested the basket on.

This boy has a list, not a severe one, no more than about five degrees, which means that he has nearly finished his round, or has a lighter-than-usual load. The boy at Melbourne Avenue is having a breather and has been captured for posterity having it. If his boss bought a copy of this card it probably caused a minor rumpus. 'I say young Perkins, I don't pay you to sit around on walls, you know'.

The inquisitive gentleman at Coombe Road, Crookes, probably did not enjoy the services of a delivery boy, for he has a wheelbarrow, evidently home made. Perhaps he is taking home the weekend joint.

These photographs also show the versatility and usefulness of the gas lamp. It could be affixed to buildings, planted in front gardens or more conventionally erected on the pavement. Gas lamps also often carried street names, gently lit from behind to inform the nocturnal wanderer. A particularly illuminating specimen, and a fine example of municipal frugality is seen on the far left. This lamp has saved the Tramway's Department the cost of erecting a proper tram stop.

Coombe Road, Crookes

This selection is specially for Sheffield people who have moved away from the city, now live in flat parts of the world, such as Lincolnshire, Holland or certain parts of Australia, and are missing the hilly streets of their native city.

How dull life must be for them. How flat.

The typical vista of old Sheffield for me is a long street on which the terraced houses have been built down the hillside in steps, so that if the people in one house look out of the top of their downstairs window they are nearly level with the bottom of the upstairs window of the house next door.

Sheffield builders had to refer to their spirit levels constantly. I bet some of them yearned to build a row of houses on a flat bit of land.

These four pictures show the kind of difficulties they faced. In fact, on the right hand side of the Walkley Lane picture, in the distance, there is a house just being built with a ladder up against it. I have no doubt whatever that the ladder has three or four blocks of wood under one leg. If it hasn't it will not stay up for long.

The odd man out of these four is the Meadowhead picture, which was taken looking up-hill from Abbey Lane. The others were taken looking down-hill.

The photographer had probably had a busy day and did not feel up to hoofing all the way up the hill. The horse, attached to the cart in the centre of the picture seems to feel the same way.

Just in front of the horse is what appears to be an old steam lorry. Either that or the cab's on fire.

Meadowhead

Brookhouse Hill, Fulwood

Sheffield's famous hills are a problem for cyclists, ladies with heavy shopping baskets and learner drivers who don't know where their handbrakes are. But they have always been very useful to photographers.

The photographer who climbed Bradway Bank captured a view of an area that was only just starting to be developed. There are a few houses on Totley Brook Road, and beyond them there is nothing but fields.

The man who took the Wincobank picture managed to get the required elevation, but unfortunately there seems to have been a lot of smoke hanging over the houses on the day he was at work.

Even so, there is enough detail to see Fife Street going up the hill, the Engineer's Hotel to the right, and a signalman, having popped out of his box to see what the photographer is up to.

The Ecclesall Road cameraman was really only half way up a hill, but perhaps he wanted to make sure that he included the Greystones Cinema in his picture.

Ecclesall Road

VIEW FROM BRADWAY BANK. 2.

After more than 130 years of operation, the last few of them under lingering threat of extinction, the Woodhead railway line between Sheffield and Manchester was finally closed this year. In its latter days it was electrified and there was a new tunnel at Woodhead, but in the early days of this century, trim little Great Central 4-4-0's like these two dashed about the line, and plunged into the old tunnel. They look very attractive, but standing in an open cab for the three miles and twenty-two yards of Woodhead tunnel must have been a bit of a trial.